What Light
There Is
&
Other Poems
by
Eamon Grennan

North Point Press
San Francisco 1989

Grateful acknowledgment is made to the editors of the following magazines, in which many of these poems first appeared: *Bellingham Review, Cyphers, Hudson River Anthology, Irish Press* (New Irish Writing), *Irish Times, Irish University Review, Literary Review, Kenyon Review, Missouri Review, Ontario Review, Ploughshares, Poetry Ireland, Poughkeepsie Review, Rostrum, Threshold, Tracks, Verse.*

"Soul Music: The Derry Air," "Incident," "All Souls' Morning," "Wing Road," "Morning: The Twenty-Second of March," "Men Roofing," and "Four Deer" appeared originally in *The New Yorker.* "Totem" appeared originally in *The Paris Review.* "At Home in Winter" and "Houseplants in Winter" appeared originally in *Poetry.*

"Night-Piece" appeared originally in *Hill Field* (St. Paul, 1989), a Festschrift for John Montague.

The poems in Part I and Part III were published in Dublin by Gallery Press: *Wildly for Days* in 1983 and *What Light There Is* in 1987. Some of these poems also appeared in *Twelve Poems* published by Occasional Works in Woodside, Calif., in 1988.

I wish also to acknowledge with gratitude the generous encouragement of the late Howard Moss.

LIBRARY OF CONGRESS
CATALOGING-IN-PUBLICATION DATA
Grennan, Eamon, 1941–
    What light there is & other poems / Eamon Grennan.
        p.   cm.
    ISBN 0-86547-370-6 — ISBN 0-86547-371-4 (pbk.)
    I. Title.   II. Title: What light there is and other poems.
PR6057.R398W48   1989
821'.914—dc19   88-37573

North Point Press
850 Talbot Avenue
Berkeley, California
94706

For Kate and Conor

Contents

PART ONE

Wildly for Days

To the memory of Tom Grennan (1910–1981)
and George Anthony Palmer (1901–1976)

Facts of Life, Ballymoney

I would like to let things be:

The rain comes down on the roof
The small birds come to the feeder
The waves come slowly up the strand.

Three sounds to measure
My hour here at the window:
The slow swish of the sea
The squeak of hungry birds
The quick ticking of rain.

Then of course there are the trees—
Bare for the most part.
The grass wide open to the rain
Clouds accumulating over the sea
The water rising and falling and rising
Herring-gulls bobbing on the water.

They are killing cuttlefish out there,
One at a time without fuss.
With a brisk little shake of the head
They rinse their lethal beaks.

Swollen by rain, the small stream
Twists between slippery rocks.
That's all there's to it, spilling
Its own sound onto the sand.

In one breath one wink all this
Melts to an element in my blood.

And still it's possible to go on
Simply living
As if nothing had happened.

Nothing has happened:
Rain inching down the window,
Me looking out at the rain.

Morning, Looking Out

Across the canal a woman in grey leans out
Her window and pours from a white jug
Over the pink sill-geraniums water
That glitters and is gone.

From the windowsill she hangs
A cage of coloured birds—rose,
Lemon and green—jittery as crickets.
Sunlight stipples them gorgeous.

The dark square of her room
Frames her, a moment, then takes her in.
Like a rainbow her laundry arches
Over the bleached green water.

Venice, October 1980

In the National Gallery, London
for Derek Mahon

These Dutchmen are in certain touch
With the world we walk on. Velvet
And solid as summer, their chestnut cows
Repeat cloud contours, lie of the land.

Everything gathers the light in its fashion:
That boat's ribbed bulging, the ripple
Of red tweed at the oarsman's shoulder;
The way wood displaces water, how water
Sheens still, the colour of pale irises.

Your eye enters this avenue
Of tall, green-tufted, spinal trees:
You tense to the knuckled ruts, nod
To the blunted huntsman and his dog,
The farmer tying vines, the discreet couple
Caught in conversation at a barn's brown angle.
You enter the fellowship of laundered light.

From the ritual conducted around this table
These men in black stare coolly back at you,
Their business, a wine contract, done with.
And on the brightly polished ice these villagers
Are bound to one another by the bleak
Intimacies of winter light—a surface laid
Open like a book, where festive and desperate
They flock like birds of passage
Between seasons, knowing the enclosing sky
Like the back of their hands, at home
In the cold, making no bones of it.

At My Sister's Flat in London

Decent the white flowers on the table
Telling the exact centre, daisies
Their bright eyes open wide
And the table laid for breakfast:
The brown bread coupled to its knife
The butter golden in a green dish
Strong tea brewing in a blue pot
Orange juice brimming a shapely glass.

Things of the ordinary morning world.
This morning luminant under low cloud
Over the tilt solidity of roofs
Their grey slates palely shining,
And in the misted distance the green
Encouraging curvature of trees.

You bless in your own abiding way
Civilities of the gardens parcelled out
To tame grass and the dazzle of roses,
These shrill swifts scything the air,
Keeping their hearts up, in every weather.

Sunday Morning Through Binoculars

Balmy as summer. It won't last.
The wind is idling somewhere
Out to sea, making its mind up.
No bells. Silence is a state of grace.
From here the farmers' cottages
Are barnacles, limewhite,
Jutting from the lumpy plum-blue hill.
For once the birds seem unwary, careless:
Meadow pipits foam out of the furze,
A lark plummets into dead heather,
Two twites perch on a grey shoulder
Of limestone. Their tiny mouths
Open and close. I suppose they're singing.
Four black whiteheaded cows
Roam in slow fat lazy waves
Over the spongy green shallows
Of their pasture. In the distance
Two boys stand knee-deep
In a platinum pond, skimming stones;
Their motions slow, deliberate as dreams.
I can't hear the stones slap water,
The water hissing, their fox-red dog's
Ecstatic barking. They step now
Gently from the water backwards
And turn to go. The Sabbath
Winking on drenched wellingtons.

Renvyle, February 1981

On a 3 ½-Ounce Lesser Yellowlegs, Departed Boston August 28, Shot Martinique September 3

for Phoebe Palmer

Little brother, would I could
Make it so far, the whole globe
Curling to the quick of your wing.

You leave our minds lagging
With no word for this gallant
Fly-by-night, blind flight.

But ah, the shot: you clot
In a cloud of feathers, drop
Dead in a nest of text-books.

Now seasons migrate without you
Flying south. At the gunman's door
The sea-grapes plump and darken.

Swifts Over Dublin

Stop, look up, and welcome these artful
Dodgers, high-flyers on the wing, these
Ecstatic swirlers, sons of air
And daring, daughters of the slow burn,
Who twist and kiss and veer, high
As kites on homecoming. Survivors,
They've put their nightsweats by,
Harrowing darkness in a rumour of wings
And companionable squeaking, riding the blast.
Now, how they celebrate a comeback, casting
High-pitched benedictions down on
Shopping-centres, stray dogs, monoxide traffic.

From any point of view they are
Beyond me, dark sparks of mystery
I must look up to, where they usher
The full flush of summer in, highly
Delighted with themselves and sporting
Their keen, seasonal dominion.

Wife

It is Spring and he brings me wildflowers
Primroses bluebells forget-me-nots
He stands them in a glass on the kitchen table
Celandine stitchwort violet ramson.
Their names make a tiny brightness—
Odours of garlic, kitchen smells.
Bright young things they shine
They shine for days.

I tidy his room and his table
I rinse the shit from our child's pyjamas
I boil rice and potatoes and porridge.
He gives me the glittering names of birds
Wheatear blackcap yellowhammer wren.
In the wind I hang out our washing:
His shirts dance, standing on their heads.

I move from room to room with brush and dustpan.
The light when it's not raining
Trails me like a child around every corner.
Behind that blind closed door I know
He is staring out his window at the clouds.
I scrape the cold ashes from the grate;
I get the new fire going.

Laundromat

In the dryer, shaken sleepers,
Their washing revives,

Spirals like kites
Flaring fabulous tails.

Sheets belly high spirits
In love with shirts

Whose empty arms embrace anything:
Hold me, they hopelessly cry,

*Wrapped up in one another
Let us never part.* They part

Breathless and headlong,
They shine like morning.

Socks, footloose and airy,
Perform prodigies of speed,

Denims tangle with corduroys
Their wild legs bucking.

Like herons the bath-towels
Flap gravely round. Handkerchiefs

Flutter like finches
Panicky at the feeder

Till their spinning sphere
Slows down, slows down, and stops.

With cold slow hands
He slaps down flat

His wife's underthings: panties,
Bras, a crinkled slip.

She beats his limp jeans
Into manageable squares. They tug

Tousled sheets straight
And fold them soberly, then

Lay all neatly out
In a plastic yellow basket

Barred as any cage.

Daughter Waiting for School Bus

She balances the frosty morning
At the jagged edge of traffic;
The winter gathers behind her
Hard grass and cracked branches.

Knees bend, hips sway, toes tap to
Some tune of her own invention;
Her body seems made of music—
She is beating time all over.

She takes from the air an air,
Making a song and dance of
Whatever passes, even the big trucks
That shake us to our foundations.

Sound as a bell she stands there,
More composed than anything I know;
The rude world enters her little body—
She returns it as music, dancing.

Taking My Son to School

His first day. Waiting, he plays
By himself in the garden.
I take a photo he clowns for,
Catching him, as it were, in flight.

All the way there in the car he chatters
And sings, giving me directions.
There are no maps for this journey:
It is the wilderness we enter.

Around their tall bespectacled teacher,
A gaggle of young ones in summer colours.
Silent, he stands on their border,
Clutching a bunch of purple dahlias,

Shyly he offers them up to her.
Distracted she holds them upside down.
He teeters on the rim of the circle,
Head drooping, a flower after rain.

I kiss him goodbye and leave him:
Stiff, he won't meet my eye.
I drive by him but he doesn't wave.
In my mind I rush to his rescue.

The distance bleeding between us,
I steal a last look back:
From a thicket of blondes, brunettes,
His red hair blazes.

It is done. I have handed him over.
I remember him wildly dancing
Naked and shining, shining
In the empty garden.

Mother and Child

for Joan

She forms a warm nest for him
Where he creeps in each morning
I'm away. Content, he curls up
Near her heat, and she slides
Head first into sleep again,
Knowing well what she's made flesh
Of her flesh, of her bone, bone.

She drifts between dreams.
She sees his red hair shining
Over the book he's propped
Upright against the mound of hip
And stretch of thigh. An early light
Finds her dark head on the pillow,
Whitens the bony wing of his arm.

All day I've carried them around
Just so, like an old photograph:
The vaulted warmth of her body lifting,
Letting gently fall the bedclothes,
Light beginning to bloom in their hair.
His grave eyes move across the page
Slowly, like loving hands.

On a Cape May Warbler Who
Flew Against My Window

She's stopped in her southern tracks
Brought haply to this hard knock
When she shoots from the tall spruce
And snaps her neck on glass.

From the fall grass I gather her
And give her to my silent children
Who give her a decent burial
Under the dogwood in the garden.

They lay their gifts in the grave:
Matches, a clothes-peg, a coin;
Fire paper for her, sprinkle her
With water, fold earth over her.

She is out of her element forever
Who was air's high-spirited daughter;
What guardian wings can I conjure
Over my own young, their migrations?

The children retreat indoors.
Shadows flicker in the tall spruce.
Small birds flicker like shadows—
Ghosts come nest in my branches.

A Gentle Art

for my mother

I've been learning how to light a fire
Again, after thirty years. Begin (she'd say)
With a bed of yesterday's newspapers—
Disasters, weddings, births and deaths,
All that everyday black and white of
History is first to go up in smoke. The sticks
Crosswise, holding in their dry heads
Memories of detonating blossom, leaf. Saved
From the ashes of last night's fire,
Arrange the cinders among the sticks.
Crown them with coal nuggets, handling
Such antiquity as behooves it,
For out of this darkness, light. Look,
It's a cold but comely thing
I've put together as my mother showed me,
Down to sweeping the fireplace clean. Lit
You must cover from view, let it concentrate—
Some things being better done in secret.
Pretend another interest but never
Let it slip your mind: know its breathing,
Its gulps and little gasps, its silence
And satisfied whispers, its lapping air.
At a certain moment you may be sure (she'd say)
It's caught. Then you simply leave it be.
It's on its own now, leading its mysterious
Hungry life, becoming more itself by the minute,
Like a child grown up, growing strange.

Common Theme

1. *Vigil*

I know nothing

Pale wasted flesh
Perplexed
And shivering from us
Spring fattens the grass
Outside his window

Remember
Last thing at night
Winter nights
Steam coiling
From the kettle's beak
Pungency of cloves
Honey and hot whiskey
Chime of the spoon
Striking glass

Now his nose sharp as a nib
Milky glaze of his eyes
A drunken look
The drugs they give him

Remember
His late key at last
Fumbling in the lock
Dull clunk of the bolt
On the kitchen door
The muffled downstairs voices
Rising and falling
In my shiver of dark

Here are his arms
Out at elbow
A heron's bony
Broken wings

Remember
The morning-after
Stillness of the house
Miracle smells
Of Sunday breakfast
Sandpaper cough
The lavatory torrent
His footsteps
A tap splashing

Here is the half-
Glass of water he
Inches to his lips
My hand in silence
Guiding his hand

Remember the Sunday
Cut-crystal glasses
Foaming
With red lemonade
The jug of clear water
Poised above the measure
Of whiskey in his fist
The splash of light

Here
Are his bleached hands
Fumbling with the sheet
Like beached starfish

2. *He Sleeps*

Into the ward slips dusk
Like a dedicated matron.
Across the deserted golf-course
A grey mist grows
Luminous among the shadowy
Stark uprights of trees
And beige craters of sand—
         like dawn, I imagine,
         coming up in China.

3. *Leaving*

Among other things
The bed, the bathroom mirror,
The clock humming on the mantelpiece,
Spectacles winking on the windowsill,
Car keys in a pewter ashtray—
Souvenir of Penn. State U.

And outside in his walled garden
A conflagration of daffodils,
One amputated apple tree,
A tenebrous bush of spring broom
Just beginning to dazzle, and
Roofing the whole thing in as usual
The perpetual tent of cloud
Tattered with seacoast mountain light.

When it comes to flesh and blood,
The most fragile things in the world
Are hard as nails
And sit there like stone creatures
Deaf and blind in a silent room
In a silent room and take no notice
When one, as he did, takes his leave.

Dublin, March 1981

21

End of Winter

I spent the morning my father died
Catching flies. They'd buzz and hum
Against the warm illuminated pane
Of the living-room window. Breathless
My hand would butterfly behind them
And cup their fear in my fist,
Their filament wings tickling
The soft centre of my palm. With my
Left hand I unlatched the window and
Opened my right wide in the sunshine.
They'd spin for a second like stunned
Ballerinas, then off with them, tiny
Hearts rattling like dice, recovered
From the fright of their lives. I watch
Each one spiral the astonishing
Green world of grass and drift
Between the grey branches of the ash.
I see each quick dark shadow
Smudge the rinsed and springing earth
That shone beyond belief all morning.
There must have been at least a dozen
I saved like that with my own hands
Through the morning, when they shook off sleep
In every corner of the living room.

Something After All

Sitting in what was my father's
And is now my mother's house I wonder
Will the mirror tell me what I have become.
Beyond the back window
The valedictory arms of the apple tree
Wave the last of their vivid spirits
At the white drift of gulls going down
From the mountains to the sea. Sunlight
Makes the vulnerable colours of the neighbourhood
Hall-doors shine. The other is the sunny
Side of the street this morning and I sit
In shadow, imagining a Chinese poet
Who sees this world through half-closed eyes
And sees nothing but apple blossom
Brushing the stem of his neck, the subtle
Stalks of his hair, and senses beyond question,
This is it. Two sparrows
Light, nibbling in the rose-bush
That claws across the garden wall. Out
Back, behind this widowed house, the wild
Broom is a holy show, menacing the mild air
With extravagant dazzle. Last month's daffodils
Have given up their lemon-headed ghosts: they are
At home in their native earth again, reposed
As one who believes in the bright life
Of blossom, fruit, falling leaf, who is at home
In the ineffable air of his own country
Between the mountains and the sea. *It is,*
He says to himself or dreams he says,
How it is. The day endures in his breath,
In the light pooling his eyes; shadows live
Like cats in the back garden, and the doors
On the sunny side of the street are shining,
If I can believe my eyes, like new leaves.

James Wright, 1927–1980

1.

It is the supple conjunction of two
Chestnut horses in a green field
And ringing them like a dish
Of spilt primordial light
A spread of mustardweed and poppies.

It is an August afternoon in which
They nuzzle one another, swanning
Their sleek necks down to kiss
This homely, native ground.

It is a steamy day and I see
Their undulant lovely forms like
Figures on a frieze, their movements
Concentrated, patient, grave.

Dusk will widen her starry eyes
To their sober appreciation,
Or new light travel their flanks
Like a warm hand, heavy with whispering.

2.

Your book crosses water with me:
Out of its fresh leaves peer
Your earthly deer and your horses;

Quail whirr away in transient panic,
The little blue heron is still
As a gravestone bird, and the fox
Paces his acres of milkweed and sleeping miners.

See where the sky blooms after rain—
Incredible feathered things

Climb and twist about the air,
Alive to its every veer and ripple.

3.
There's an old Irish
Poem about death: *A house*
Where rain won't fall
A fearless place
Open as a garden
Without a wall around it.

And *the secret of this journey*, you said,
Meaning life, meaning death,
Is to let the wind
Blow its dust all over your body.

Certain as a chestnut pony
You step away
To *the heart of the light.*

Source

A narrow passage
Where the moist
Moss-covered stones
Barely glimmer

A shimmering dark
I would willingly enter

A cool brimming
Shivers
With what's possible

Stillness of spirit
And in the distance
Flute-voiced water.

Mushroom-Picking in the Old World

Remember the soft morning: moist, pulpy, odorous
With cow-dung, drenched grass, blackberry leaves,
The damp seeping into your shoes, your toes
At home in it. You haul yourself over the stone wall
And enter the field you've been told in secret:
A secret field, where they spend their secret lives.

Your parents still asleep. Do it at dawn,
They tell you, hour of their flowering. *Fás aon oíche,*
Starlit children of a single night. Breathless,
Your eyes go squirrelling the grass. The milk-can, from
Your hand dangling, bright as a new sixpence,
The morning seal-grey, a barely luminous stir about you.

You feel their foreign heartbeat through the grass:
They are a firm spongy fullness in the hand, a rich
Smell overwhelming the house, a blessing of boiled milk
And garlic. The phrase, *fruits of the earth*, fires
In your head. Stark moons, out of the mothering dark
Into the moment of your hands they've swollen.

You trace their charmed circle on your knees, touching
Each one gently, cap and stem, before you break it.
Remember the deep clean silence, the lover's concentration.
In no time, the can overflows with their clod-mottled
Ivory flesh and you go. At the kitchen table
Your mother will string them, big beads, to wrinkle dry.

Muse, Maybe

You are never at home with her:
She shies the familiar touch.
Lady of half-lights,
You cannot make her out from shadows.

There's no catching up with her:
She sleeps near your sleep;
Your mind wears her face like a mask.
She is the lady of changes.

She's the girl you kissed in the graveyard,
Hers the warm skin under a raincoat.
You turned sixteen that winter, speechless
At heart, for all your speeches.

She wears the air of what's possible,
Making your pulse ache. *Find me out,*
She says, *put me in the clear.*
You've made such promises before.

Stuffed Birds

They abide my tactless curiosity.
—Things have been, they seem to say,
Desperately narrowed down. Can you
Call back the mountain air for us,
Broken by big wings, or the moist
Comfort of reeds at evening, or
Nervy with generation the giant grass
Where we shrieked and fiercely tumbled,
Loving and hunting one another down?
Eagle, hawk, and totem owl,
Gaudy warbler, woodcock, wren—
We're migrant now beyond desire,
Keeping our caged and outraged peace.
Discriminate in the business of living,
We've grown promiscuous in death.
We have come to perpetual attention,
Confined to your flights of fancy
And our passive infinitive—*to be seen*.
Brief epitomes of quickness,
To you we are signs and portents
Making a show of ourselves, breeding fear.

The light outside is riddled with birds
Earnest about their everyday mysteries.
They call to one another from behind
The fringed willow drapes, kiss themselves
In the lake's live glass, then rise
Out of my sight into an air
Of nerves and arteries where daylight
Pulses and will not stay.

Speech

Like learning a strange tongue.

You spend years half-mastering
Its curious inflections,
Learning its moods by heart.
The tug and swirl of
Alien idioms try you
With their own home truths.

You practise it daily,
Prize your own fluency,
Admire the sentiments that
Suffer in translation, find
A few with a reading knowledge.

You chance one day
On a native speaker
And startle into silence,
Struck dumb by a speech
That makes sense at last.

Now you're quiet as an owl,
Ears cupped and padded
To catch the smallest sound—
Titter of leaf, whisper of grass,
Static of dead sticks. You

Daydream perfect conversations—
The brown fieldmouse
Fast asleep
In the hushed, unruffled
Cradle of your beak.

Cavalier and Smiling Girl

Vermeer

The Old World geography
Of their proximate bodies
Odysseys beyond the actual
Map and gaping window:
They have discovered one another.

Ordinary water glistens
Where her linked fingers
Follow the curve of the glass:
This, she knows, is something
Elemental to hold onto.

Here is heart's cartography
Toying with absence,
Making of great space
A shapely consolation—
A picture of projected grief.

No grief in this luminous
Mortal minute, this little room
Where her indigenous smile
Fixes something between them—
Making light of her life.

Voices

We live in shadows and the shadows live
Peremptory questioning lives
Together in that house again again
With its weeping walls. Who was it
Heard the voice in the pear tree,
The voice in the kitchen cupboard,
The strict voice between the sheets
Sounding between his lips and the kissed nipple:
Give your old name up
Throw your robe around your shoulders
Take a staff of wood, a wooden bowl,
Kiss your wife goodbye.

Whose was the voice in my head
When I watched a spider feel
His delicate way up glass in a trap of shadows
Where the big linden darkens your window,
The voice reciting the hundred words for snow
The hundred words for grass, the words
For the unimaginable sadness of mammals
Going blind, the weird wide space of their patience
As they stumble for somewhere to die? What
Do they say at last? I lie awake at night
Now, listening to the sounds the house makes
Whispering its rosary of comforts against the wind.
No knowing the hour the voice will choose
To make a listener of me.

Fall

On a still morning the shallow pond
Is full of kissing: little narcissi—
Sandpiper sanderling killdeer plover—
Dip to their brilliant twins
In the motionless water. Egrets connect
Exactly with their own stealthy brightness,
Uncoil their slow snake-necks and come
Within an inch of the water's skin
And enter. Unsteady rings ride out
From these feathered centres, each bird
Making its presence felt, heartfelt
Quick solidity at the heart of things.

And patiently gazing at themselves
In the mirroring water
The flowers of the season
Murmur their own sufficient names—
Touch-me-not loosestrife forget-me-not—
Lovers of the clear pool, the crisp morning.

Fragrance of ripe apples in the air.
Savour of honey in the empty mouth.

Skunk

Night brims with his bittersweet.
Sometimes a squashed body does it. For miles
The highway blows his grief among the trees.
Other times it's fear burns that incense
In the dark. Or it could be just delight—
Two of them finding one another,
Slow and curious
Among moist ferns and cool bluegreen shadows.
Black and white, warm as saliva.
Infinitely, as such things go, desirable.
They make no secret of what's between them:
Hanging their lavish presence on the night,
They scatter anarchy in pungent waves
Through the dark outside your bedroom window.

Lying Low

The dead rabbit's
Raspberry belly
Gapes like a mouth;

Bees and gilded flies
Make the pulpy flesh
Hum and squirm:

O *love*, they sing
In their nail-file voices,
We are becoming one another.

His head intact, tranquil,
As if he's dreaming
The mesmerised love of strangers

Who inhabit the red tent
Of his ribs, the radiant
Open house of his heart.

By the Hudson

My dear, in the dead of winter
You see from the train window
Yellow light and white mist
Melt into one another on the water.

Hundreds of wintering ducks
Swim in the light like shades,
And you wish to think of dying like this,
Only living keeps getting in the way.

This is the sort of morning you are
In my mind—a complicated light
That is quick with shadows, bright mist
In which our life and death lie wintering.

Winter

Who, when they are all gone, will
You be to yourself? You swallow air
Like ether edged with razor-blades
And run squeaking over the frozen snow.

Summer was like love and marriage:
You could scarcely see the cold
Coming through the haze of fat grass
And flesh. You wake and find it's done for.

This weather brings us to our senses.
Pity the fox, the melancholy badger,
The fieldmouse clean as a snowflake,
Shivering and praying in the flayed hedges.

Trees After Snow

In white the trees are languishing
Like Victorian brides, their ever-
Green bodies bowed beneath the cold
Weight. *This is not what we were told,*
They think, imagining apple-blossom.

Bearing the weight of weather
They too have their breaking point,
Though they mostly stand or soar
In their own image, and their arms
Are wonderful, midsummer, with birds.

22 December 1981

Night Driving in the Desert

Move fluent as water
Splashing brightness. Imagine
Jackal badger wild goat,
Fox-eyes glinting like broken glass:
Gingerly they sniff the sour exhaust.
Remember greenness; name
Its distant children: *ryegrass*
Olive avocado fig—
Sweetness welling in the mouth.
Herbs the Arabs call *ashab*
Sprout under a single rain
Rush to blossom fruit seed
Staining the sand with rainbows.
Imagine a procession of tanager dresses
Drifting through coppergreen shadow—
Women moving like water over the earth
Sunlight splashing their skin to stars.
I know it is over in a flash and after
My heart is beating wildly, wildly for days.

Raeburn's Skater

I want his delicate balance, his
Sturdy sane domesticated grace.

Arms crossed, he holds himself together,
Equilibrist of spirit, solid nerve.

Crowblack and solemn he lives at a tilt
Between limegreen ice and coral air.

Beyond his ken, out of the picture,
The fixed stars hold him fast.

Armageddon Autumn

Wherever you walk
These weeks of polished amber
Of burn and burnish
Invisible bird-dash
(How they quicken their farewells)
Patches of sudden light
Fall in your path

Like friendly visitants
From a distant world
Who have back home discovered
The secret of peace,
Making radiant the skin of
Grey beech, maple, flayed sycamore,
Turning stone walls gold.

We've been provided for,
It seems, though underground
The neutron bulbs
Doze in their cast-iron cradles
And it all boils down
To this: what
We can do to one another

Though we've seen the light.

For the Record

After six unsparing days of storm
A grey still day without rain.
Nothing spectacular, no exploding
Stars off the lake, no precious
Glitter of soaked grass, no triumph
In bannering branches, just branches
Taking the air as if it belonged
To them, the faint sleepy chink-
Chink of the robin in the next field,
And everything back in its place.
But nothing carnival or sabbatical,
Only a sort of steady domestic peace
Secures all animations in the garden,
Giving everything its due. No fuss,
No unexpected flares, no amazing
Grace in the play and swift trans-
Figurings of light off water. Only
Cloud, seamless still air, this hush.
So, after six days of storm, record
A perfectly ordinary day at last—
Dry; a little on the cool side.

PART TWO

A Single Window

Night-Piece

What's that scratching
at the sweet young bones
of my son and daughter?

I kiss them goodnight
and shut my ears; they turn
their bones to me and laugh.

You cry out in sleep
and rise up stiffly pointing:
What's that that at the window?

I see where your blind eyes
anchor. *Nothing, nothing love*
but the moon setting fire

to the hummingbirds
and wild roses. The house
stares out at the dark, at itself

staring blindly back. Downstairs
the furniture crouches
like trapped cats; the blackout

fireplace gapes. In a lit upper window
of the house across the street
that woman's body burns

like a comet: back, buttock, thigh
one incandescent curve; breasts
a wave cresting. My broken image

a ghost in the glass. Nameless
are the hills and water-bodies
that hold us here. The stars

roost on our rooftops or in the empty
nest of branches, their distant names
a glitter: Vega, Aldebaran, Betelgeuse—

all the brilliant winter
constellations—and Berenice's
Hair. My children grind their teeth

in sleep: they dream being lost
in an earthquake, between the city
and the sea. I am that absence

they sense around their hearts,
that wedding ring of frost
noosing the moon. The sea storms

under a sky bristling with
shrapnel; houses come tumbling: long
crooked scars of light

open every wall. I know now
what troubled those dear bones
in sleep. Night creeps by.

March

Spare, stripped down, glows
With its own hard light. Clean
Speed in its fits and starts, in
Its shifty winds, cloud ceilings,
Darkened afternoons, lucid intervals.

Short, exhausted, frost-blenched—the grass
Knows it must be nothing first, then
Absolution. Light shivers
In the ribbed scaffolding of trees.

It is a world of wind-lit bones
Grown brisk, articulate in prophecy
And loss, the strict truth audible
In diehard tongues of quartz. Sleek
Snakes of water, after a day's rain,
Weave across the cellar floor; big
Wings of eastern early light
Batter the attic window. Everything
Pared to a point of tense repose, the self
Speaking simply for itself at last.

Drop by deliberate cloudwater drop
The maple sap slips into the lidded
Bucket. Lemonyellow, amber, black,
A flapdance of bathtowels flexes
On the clothesline, side by side
Like Greeks. In this month's book
Of changes, I read my father's end
Again: how from his bed he watched
The hoarse rooks build in chestnut trees
And ruined elms their rowdy mansions,
How as day beat after day he saw the rain
And all its shadows break to shine.

Patience in Renvyle

These brown cows colour the path
I go down to the house.
Their huge heads nuzzle tufts.

A couple of good green years
Of grass and weather-smells
They're sure of, then the hard knock.

It is, I tell myself, a sort of life:
Keeping the earth in place,
Holding the sky over their heads.

Fields and lumpy fields spread out
From their ponderous bodies:
A frieze of foreign meanings.

Light sharpens and grows hard.
My long evening shadow
Cuts between them like a knife.

Porridge

While you're cooking breakfast
I follow the thread of its smell
back to that first kitchen where
porridge bubbled on the aster-
blue petals of gas. Bland and
mealy as flour sacks, the smell
used to snake upstairs to where I
find myself, half dressed, shivering
before the electric fire's redgold stems
that buzz in blueberry tiles and glow
like the statue of the Sacred Heart.

Coffeedark was my father's
morning scent, cigarette smoke
and the acrid black of toast
scorching under the grill. The sharp
rasp of his knife scraped burnt bits
off, butter on: a smell of charcoal
mixed with honeyed gold. Tea
was what the rest of us drank: no
smell unless I dipped my head, felt
steam wreathing cold cheeks, my
nose opening with the word *Ceylon*
—delicate as the bone china
tea-set with applegreen leaf
we used only on Sundays or for
visitors. Sniffing into the cup
like that, I'd picture my mother
bowed above the smokey basin
of Friar's Balsam, madonnaed
by a blue bath-towel, her breathing
a rich mix of phlegm and prayers
for a speedy recovery; the bedroom

a dispensary stew of wintergreen, camphor,
menthol, blackcurrant, Vick's.

If I was up first, I'd cat-pad downstairs
in stocking feet, ease the halldoor open
to bring in the milk I'd heard the milkman
clunk on the porch, empties clinking
at his finger-ends. It was beginning
to brighten: the milk shone white as milk
in its slender bottles, and the *clop clop*
of the milkman's horse, loose harness
jingling, passed up Clareville Road.
Morning smelled frost, a cut-crystal scent
that said another world existed—clean-
cold, intricate as a frozen snowflake,
somehow parallel to ours—hazardous
and dazzling and moonlit-fixed forever.
Sometimes a fresh olivebrown horseturd
smoked on the empty street like a
burnt offering, its racy breath a summer-
pungent mix of oats and meadowgrass
inflaming our tame suburban air. Frost
stiffened filaments in my nose, crinkled
the leftover roses, salted the lawn.
Kitchen smells seeped
from the house behind me. Hugging
the four cold bottles to my chest
I'd heel the halldoor shut and hurry
to pour on my porridge the creamy
top of the milk—rich, delicious,
forbidden—before my mother or my father
saw me: smells of sugar, cream, and porridge
marry, and I take that wonder in
like nothing special, till here and now
I hear you tell me from our kitchen
that breakfast's ready, and I rise
to join you, my head swimming.

The Futility of Wishing

I have wanted to be a child again
Only once, early this January morning,
More snow threatening the yellow house
I'm visiting, the woods, the winding
Back roads of western Massachusetts,
The white, stump-spired Baptist church
And the ramshackle single store
At the cross-roads, its rose Mobil Pegasus
Nailed to a gable. Through a sliver
Of bone-white blind I see
In the albumen seven-o'clock light
A small boy dressed in a down jacket,
Electric-blue, and rusty woolen cap
Set out for school. He picks
Deliberate steps, head bent, his eyes
On the cobbled frozen snow, a brown
Schoolbag on his back. Through the narrow
Gulley between ploughed drifts he moves
As if in meditation. Behind him
A patched dog—liverish yellow daubs
On dirty white—plods nodding
Through the snow. Ahead of him
Ravel fifty years of mostly speechless
Struggle with the seasons, the fevers
And chills of adolescence, the marriage
Ache, fug of smoke and hopeless talk
In the local bar—*Sue Ann's, Log
Cabin Lounge,* or *Hunter's Rest*—the endless
Loving wrestle with engines. But good
To be him this morning moment, day
Cracking open like an egg around me,
The bleached smoke-swirl of breath
Briefly staining the air
Under my nose, the huge barked beams

Stacked outside the sawmill across the road,
Raw wood colours gleaming
In ricepaper light. Biscuit-brown
Hangover oakleaves rattling
On the live trees, the first snowflakes
Feathering down the stiff folds and
Aquamarine ice-drapes of the stunned
Waterfall. Good enough to be ten years old
This minute, making my way to school
In a place I'd know as home, and not
This naked forty-two-year-old shivering
Behind a winter window, the whole place
Still strange to me. To be walking to school
While the snowbound world sleeps, the sweet
Flutter of Friday nerving my blood
Against the cold, only the dulled crunch
Of my wool-lined boots and the whispering
Pad of my companion's clotted paws
Breaking the great silence.

Eos

for R. K.

Silence. Then the clap of her hands.
Wings of the woodpigeon breaking cover:
Fear beating in the pulse of flight.

She draws darkness off like a dress.
Invisible, she makes her presence felt
In rose petals, beech leaves, blades of grass.

Amber, carnelian, lemon: brightness
Spills from her loose hair and settles
Shivering on the dark gnarl of bark, like moths.

She strides over the sea in
Whispers, coaxing rock moss from its starlit
Soft sleep, shedding bird-cries and

Perpetuity. Under her hazel eyes, the clouds
Flower—enormous magnolia blossoms that
Spread their breathtaking sex

In water. Where she walks, green birds
Stammer and separate and burn
In the bite of their present tense, shaking

Wet feathers out like fresh leaves. Say
She makes the morning happen, puts us
On common ground again, showing

No more than is there before us. Daylight's
Yet unfreckled body, she hurries among us—
One small shadow sleeping in her arms.

From Your Window

A figuring of pigeons
Corbels the roof-edge opposite:
Dark feathered hearts
Against this milky morning sky.

Two of them kissing: very
Deft their nibbling strike.
Necks snake one another:
Sheer coil of warmth.

They've come to know something
Deep about the morning—
I can almost taste it
Though there's glass between us.

They shift, as if at a signal,
Turning from one another:
The silent tide of light
Splitting them up for flight.

Still it happened.
No matter the arrogant fan and
Swirl of them taking the air,
Their inhuman and exalted stir:

For a moment they were on foot
As we are, on a lit edge
As we are—provable,
Precarious, just in touch.

Accidents

Life is not a walk across a field.
                    Pasternak

Two in one day show the cold depths
sharking under that thin ice
we've raised our lives on. Another
inch or so, we'd be statistics. Laughing
like drunks, we tell ourselves it could
be worse: I imagine firemen straining
to cut Kate out, where the truck's huge mudguard
could have crushed her door, pinned her
in her unicorn shirt and new school jacket
to the seat. Or I see you and me
as we almost were, struck at speed and
splashing through the windscreen
in a shower of glass, faces breaking
to blossom as the blood thrusts, pulses.

This could have been the case, we say,
knowing the indifferent teeth that could
have closed on us like a cat
padding into shadows, a small shape
jerking and lolling in its jaws. And later,
while I make our bed or rake the grate out,
I'm struck by how survivors go back
to these simple acts—like water settling
after a squall—go over it all while the kettle
sings into steam and the tea-leaves fall
like black confetti in the pot. You taste
the emptiness fresh, after the body
with its six or seven wounds has been
handed from the wet street into the grave,
after the fever, chill, or lingering
has done its job, when the days come back
and the nights ticking with habit. You
remember how the world shuddered a second

then went still, how the hook-beaked
bird of change came flapping and clattering
through the kitchen window in a blizzard
of arrowy shards, or just brushed lightly
with his big wings so you felt the north
wind of his breath, glimpsed the livid
ember of his unlidded eye and he was
gone.

     After two accidents less serious
than they might have been, you go back
to your daily life struck dumb—with wonder,
I want to say, but it's not that, only
the ground, knuckled with frost, seems
more solid than ever, my feet beating it
seem steadier, and I'm all at once all there,
knowing it's all a merciful fiction, that
truth is thin ice too flimsy for shadows,
that our lives hang on balances too delicate
to ponder for long as we zigzag, all eyes,
over the open field where the mines are lying.

The Cycle of Their Lives

All day, now that summer's come, the children
Drift by my window on their bicycles. Hour
After aimless hour a small bright school of them
Circles the block, nonchalant as exotic fish
That barely ruffle the avocado depths
Of a home aquarium. For the most part
Their pace is regular—pedalling the rise,
Cresting the turn, then floating dreamy-eyed
Back down. Without warning, one will break
The circle, flash off on his own, on her own,
The way they'll leave at last the homes
They'll home to. If they see me staring
Out at them from behind this glass
They wave in passing—one hand jerky in air,
Eyes colliding with mine an instant—then
Steadying a slight wobble they resume their
Instinct's occupation, drawing order from
The tangle of their lives. Morning to night
They're at it, while the gold-spoked sun
Rides the blue rim of sky, and light sifts
Through the hushed underwater web
Of leaves, altering the air they swim in
—Silvergreen, oriole, buttercup, verdigris-yellow.
Come mealtimes, their dreaming spell
Is snapped by the cries of mothers: names
Ring round the neighbourhood like bells, bringing
Each one headlong home. Indoors they fret over
Vegetables, their propped bikes glittering
Against steps and porches, the road
A pool of light and silence. The spangled
Green crosshatch of leaves hangs still. Soon
They are back in their scented kingdom, lords
Of all its lit dimensions, circling perpetually
The square. Given our condition, they fashion

57

A provisional perfect freedom, beautifully doing
Nothing, unravelling and ravelling themselves
In time, being only motion alone, savouring
The sweet empty presence of themselves
In sunlight. My own son is among them
Until lingering grey traces of air and muffled light
Cling to his white t-shirt and he glows
Almost chromium or wild white rose. When I
Call him in at last, he glimmers away for one
More turn in watery dusklight, then freewheels
Slowly towards the garage dark, dismounts, lays
His bike aside. Grounded, he trudges through
Ankle-deep grass, talking in low tones
To his friends who know their own time is
Almost come and cycle on, flickering
The way I've seen seagulls flicker, who call out
To one another as they wheel round the infinite
High reaches of the evening sky.

Woodchuck

A low brown ghost,
He ducks and umbles fatly off
Into the underbrush at my approach,
Cracking dead branches, bringing
A snow of crab apple blossom down
About his keen ears: in my head
I hear his heart thump blubbery ribs.
We share this ragpatch of land
Between houses, under a cache of
Leaf-years, the morning croon of doves,
Ululation of jays in the high locust.

He's gone from sight to ground, into
The glimmering spinach-green space
That spring and the imminence of summer
Have brimmed with yellow celandine, white
Mustard garlic, the mild erotic pinks
Of phlox and wild geranium. Entering
Those braided depths—to dump with
The rest of the dead my arm-loads of
Cut grass, spiny prunings of rosebush and
Supple young locust—I stop, listen a minute
For his husk and scuffling in the fragrant
Silence. I know he's frozen his tracks
To hark at my foreign blundering about
His dwelling place, and I feel a hair-
Trigger thorn of fear flutter in my
Throat: what if he snaps from cover,
Clasps an ankle, won't unsnag at the
Screech and salt blood staining
His teeth, won't let go this once
For all his lumped, crumpled brothers
On the highway's verge, at the lip
Of ditches? By nature pacifist, of course

He doesn't, but hunkers in his shell
Of silence and shadow, listening
To the air unravel its spool of
Family secrets, until I'm gone and his
Kind of peace settles, nesting. I bundle
My bristling armful on the heap, then
Leave this ragged green breathing space
To his stolid, spectral self, the harboring
Coil of his homeland fattening round him.

The Nature of America

Things are getting out of hand. Mornings
I come awake to the catbird's manic gabble
Scolding in broken music himself or the
Savage world he lives in. Day is one wide arm
Of buttery green tattooed with leaf-shadow;
Everything fattens into its summer body. Cats
Stalk any flicker, killing old hungers, or
Sprawl slack-jawed on the grass where tall
Bold milky stems of blown dandelions stand
In armies, and a few wild pansies flare
Cream lipped and priested purple in a simmering
Shallow sea of green. The pond across the road
Is scummed with ravenous algae, rimmed rust rose
With seeds of the red ash that leafs its raw head
Above the water. All day a persistent ticking
Of maple wings agitates the porch screen as they
Flock in hundreds, seeking their square inch
Of earth, a prodigal future. Scabbed by sunlight,
Middens of fresh trash hump in front of
Every house on the block: splayed chairs bristle,
Blind TVs gape, rustburnt bikes and drunken dolls
Beseech the dark to hide their shame, hush up
The dead child crying. Sofas put impotent springs
On show; mattresses, like mine fields, discover
The draggled ends of love. Books elbow
A passage through plastic sacks; bright shards
Of broken mirrors beam their own bad luck
At the passing world. These heaps dream of
Taking root on the wet tongue of ditches
Or winding up wooden fences while they wait
For the spring collection, which may get round to them
Before the long arms of ivy, bindweed, grapevine
Can drag them off, before they disappear down the
Open green throat of grass. Things are

Getting out of hand: always this blurred, slurring,
Sudden rush to summer, this surge of mindless green
Bellowing—*Out of my way! I drown the mountain,
Overwhelm the valley! Beat my funeral bell
For your puny suburbs!*—we and the increasing air
All thunderstruck. And this is why whole hills,
Wide valleys, plains of shaking grass are rooted
Up, laid flat, swept from sight and mind—for
Fear the delicate zealous fingers of the willow
Will take us by the throat, the patient soft moss
Shut our eyes up; for fear we'll smother, crying out
In a dervish of roots, leaves, abandoned blossom.

Winn's Blackbird

for Winn and Larry Smith

Drawn out of the oven's dark,
He's laid to rest on the kitchen table.
Every feather dry as a leaf;
He's nested with death all winter.

You take the shutters down. Summer
Beats white wings in every corner:
The big light broods on familiar objects;
The house hatches round his final silence.

For you, he's the dead you live with:
Your friends, your blood, your buried women.
You welcome him to your painter's eye and
Day by day make him articulate again.

Each sketch an act of faith: death
Is what you're giving life to. In your favorite
He seems almost buoyant—charcoal neck
Stretched with a sense of purpose.

At dinner, remembering the dead we share,
We five fall silent, letting them enter. You say
There's a life in things outgrows our knowing.
The drenched grapes, the strawberries, glitter

Like stars. Out in the studio (dark as an oven),
Adjusting to the status of all caught things,
The finished sketches sleep. But
Your bird, imagine, takes flight.

Vespers

Back they flash at dusk
Incandescent shards of starlight
Scorching the silent grass.

Hedge-dwelling hungry birds
Morsels of unimaginable dread
Dashed against the garden's peace.

Desperate the intent wren
Wild-eyed among the rushes
Shaking twilight from his vexed wings

Searches for something, something,
Hightailing it for cover. *Where,*
Where is it? Where is it?

PART THREE

What Light There Is

For Rachel

Wing Road

Amazing, how the young man who empties
our dustbin ascends the truck as it moves
away from him, rises up like an angel
in a china-blue check shirt and lilac
woollen cap, dirty work-gloves, rowanberry
red bandanna flapping at his throat. He plants
one foot above the mudguard, locks his
left hand to a steel bar stemming
from the dumper's loud mouth and is borne
away, light as a cat, right leg dangling,
the dazzled air snatching at that black-
bearded face. He breaks to a smile, leans
wide and takes the morning to his puffed
chest, right arm stretched far out, a checkered
china-blue wing gliding between blurred earth
and heaven, a messenger under the locust trees
that stand in silent panic at his passage. But
his mission is not among the trees: he has
flanked both sunlit rims of Wing Road
with empty dustbins, each lying on its side,
its battered lid fallen beside it, each
letting noonlight scour its emptiness
to shining. Carried off in a sudden cloud
of diesel smoke, in a woeful crying out
of brakes and gears, a roaring of monstrous
mechanical appetite, he has left this unlikely
radiance straggled behind him, where the crows,
covening in branches, will flash and haggle.

Incident

for Louis Asekoff

Mid-October, Massachusetts. We drive
through the livid innards of a beast, dragon
or salamander, whose home is fire. The hills
a witch's quilt of goldrust, flushed cinnamon,
wine fever, hectic lemon. After dark, while
water ruffles, salted, in the big pot, we four
gather towards the woodfire, exchanging
lazy sentences, waiting dinner. Sunk
in the supermarket cardboard box
the four lobsters tip and coolly stroke each other
with rockblue baton legs and tentative
antennae, their breath a wet clicking, the undulant
slow shift of their plated bodies
like the doped drift of patients
in the padded ward. Eyes like squished berries
out on stalks. It's the end of the line
for them, yet faintly in that close-companioned air
they smell the sea, a shadow-haunted hole to hide in
till all this blows over.
                                    When it's time,
we turn the music up to nerve us
to it, then take them one by one and drop
in the salty roil and scald, then clamp
the big lid back. Grasping the shapely fantail
I plunge mine in headfirst and feel
before I can detach myself the flat slap
of a jackknifed back, glimpse for an instant
before I put the lid on it
the rigid backward bow-bend of the whole body
as the brain explodes and lidless eyes
sear white. We two are bound in silence
till the pot-lid planks back and music
floods again, like a tide. Minutes later
the four of us bend to brittle pink intricate

shells, drawing white sweet flesh
with our fingers, sewing our shroud-talk
tight about us. Later, near moonless midnight,
when I scrape the leafbright broken remains
into the garbage-can outside, that last
knowing spasm eels up my arm again
and off, like a flash, across the rueful stars.

Lunch-Break on the Edge of Town

Overhead, a mile up from where we share
our sandwiches and apple cider, five slow hawks
lazily gyre on the blank blue page
of haze, loving their air and elevation. Do they
see the two of us as the same slow mobile dots
that they are, our strolling motions
among April's tattered half-green hedges
as otherworldly and deliberate as theirs? We hear
a song sparrow or a yellow warbler, invisible
in cattails behind the radio station. Elegant
as Calder-work, slim masts steel to a great
height, beaming punk love and heavy metal
into cars, into sunlit kitchens, all across
the Hudson Valley. From their own spectacular height
the hawks look down: bleak wild eyes on fire,
they murmur little gritty companionable queryings
to one another between thermals, tugs of hunger,
deaths. When our lunch is done we return to the car
and turn for town: in front of us
the arch tan body of an otter
—beige tail trimmed in black—crosses
the gravel road without haste or delay. He bears
the light of day at the twitching tips of his pelt as he
takes himself over a bank beginning to green
and into the shadowglitter and familiar reaches
of his trees near water. We stop, watching, till he's
gone, then drive in silence past the first houses.

Soul Music: The Derry Air

A strong drink, hundred-year-old
schnapps, to be sipped at, invading
the secret places that lie in wait and
lonely between bone and muscle, or
counting (Morse code for insomniacs)
the seconds round the heart
when it stutters to itself. Or to be
taken in at the eyes in small doses,
phrase by somatic phrase, a line
of laundry after dawn, air clean as
vodka, snow all over, the laundry
lightly shaking itself
from frigid sleep. Shirts, flowered sheets,
pyjamas, empty trousers, empty
socks—risen as at a last day's dawn
to pure body, light as air. Whiteness
whiter than snow, blueness bluer than
new day brightening the sky-lid
behind trees stripped of their illusions
down to a webbed geometry
subtler than speech. A fierce blue eye
farther off than God, witnessing
house-boxes huddled together
for comfort, that blindly front
the deserted streets down which in time
come farting lorries full of soldiers.
You are a fugitive *I*, a singing
nerve: you flit from garden to garden
in your fit of silence, bits of you
flaking off in steam and sizzling
like hot fat in the snow. Listen
to the pickers and stealers, the shots,
man-shouts, women wailing, the cry of kids
who clutch stuffed dolls or teddy bears

and shiver, gripping tight as a kite
whatever hand is offered. Here
is the light glinting on top-boots, on
the barrel of an M-16 that grins, holding
its hidden breath, beyond argument. And here
is a small room where robust winter sunlight
rummages much of the day when the day is
cloudless, making some ordinary potted plants
flower to your surprise again, again,
and again: pink, anemic red, wax-white
their resurrection petals. Like hearts
drawn by children, like oiled arrowheads,
their unquestioning green leaves seem
alive with expectation.

Houseplants in Winter

Their survival seems open to question.
I make a mess of watering, prune
without discretion, grieve over the leaf
whose borders burn and curl. Their
fresh petals always surprise me—
tiny coral hearts, milk-white stars.

I've lined them up on the table
I work and eat at, facing the small window
that faces almost south, setting myself
under the pale sway of their silence. In our
cramped common quarters I see them
play out their deaths, their resurrections.

I watered and watered the rose-geranium
till its roots grew bog-black, sodden:
nothing could keep its sweetness
in our lives. The jade, for all
its parakeet-green shoots and early promise,
wouldn't root: its leathery heads bowed down.

The rest seem busy getting by. Moved
to the margins of our noisy mealtimes
when my children visit, they grow used
to the smell of bread frying in goosefat
for breakfast, small talk, the after-
dinner pungency of a peeled tangerine.

This speechless life they lead is
Greek to me: when live flowers rise
out of dead heads, I reckon it's as
much for the moment as I need
to know. The light that falls on them
strikes me too, till I feel as rooted

as I'll ever be in this home
from home. Look at us, they seem to say,
flourishing under straitened circumstance:
you see we make do with your handfuls
of earth, your cups of water, these daily
visitations of winter light that cast our
impeccable shadows on your razed page.

Staying in Bed

We lay all morning talking. The window
brightens, November-grey to knife-edge blue where
Sunday becomes itself, all bells, without us. The air
flickers, blinks, riddled with starling shadows
or the brusque impulsive blobs of sparrows
flung by hunger. This one touch of winter
makes us face a few home truths: we have to enter
the cold zone naked. Sleepwalker steady, our slow

voices cross the little space between us;
companionable, our bodies stretch. Our sex
idles, half-asleep, a summer stream
flooding with fernlight green as
early wheat. Such peace: we could be dreaming
away one another's past, digesting hard facts.

Father in Front of a Picture

Vermeer's girl leans her sleeping head
on the neat curve of a wristbone, her
propped elbow taking the weight. Warm
fleshlight and lived-in familial shade
share the open doorway and watch over her
like a father, I imagine, while she snatches
brief sleep, and dreams he'll be
standing in her light when she wakes.

This agate-keen December day—a few
green streaks of grass breaking the bleak
amnesia of snow; nuthatches, finches,
chickadees quick as spring in the famished
branches—I must imagine how my own two children
will grow to know my absence
like a hint of pipe tobacco fading
as you enter a familiar room, like
a light on the landing gone out before you've
quite dropped into sleep and you lie
alone in the dark and know the dark
disputed borders of yourself, your self,
for the first time. How their sleep-warm

skin shivered when I came home
cold from my early-morning walks
this time of year, nuzzling them awake
with my rimey beard and the names of birds
I'd seen—a frost-edge glitter of wingtip
and tailfeather springing to sudden life in that
drowsy room. No knowing whether they'll
ever remember such mornings, now we're

separate, or know only my absence like
warm light bulging an open doorway while
they wish themselves to sleep, to dream
me there watching them all night until they wake
and with their own eyes find me, large as life.

Walking to Work

The trees along College Avenue stand
quiet as cows in wet weather, immense
breaths steaming, dark hides
dripping into March. Limegold,
a smear of lichen brightens
each ridged, shingled bark. Clean
as fresh paint, the nib of a first crocus
pricks silken purple from a tuft
of drained, grit-stained, faded grass.

In the painted square of some Dutch or
Northern city—Haarlem, Düsseldorf, The
Hague—a seamless shawl of light is falling
over housefronts and plump green trees, the
thin white stork on her gable-nest, over
the canal bridge where a procession of
horsemen is passing two fair-haired boys
and three sleek dogs, brick-pink. One boy
bears a perch of hooded hawks aloft. Passing

forever through this early light
to the open fields, they are leaving behind
unruffled squares, sleeping houses, still water
glistening between tidy sun-splashed banks. Were
there another life I'd be content
to spend a slice of it in such a scene—
waking at this lit hour and walking out,
loitering on the bridge to watch the men
from the big house go by: I smell their
horses' mealy sweat; their pungent hawks;
the nipping, moss-edged scent of water.

But now I am walking to work
along College Avenue in Poughkeepsie, under

a dripping braid of naked branches. High
above my head a saltwhite spindrift shimmering
of gulls: hungry yellow eyes cast down,
they've followed the river this far
from the reach of salt, bringing with them
a hint of our back garden in Dublin, my father
tossing leftover scraps in the grass and
watching those wide white copewings flap
and batter. They'd open their throats to
chicken bones, potato skins, lamb fat, brown
crusts of bread, then cast implacable heads
back, wailing. Such anarchy and appetite
dazzled his slow, encumbered blood; his
silent tongue would sting
with their otherworldly, heartless salt.

I am walking to work under sodden
branches. Any day now, spring
will take the ground, the trees, the air, our eyes
by storm. Harbouring here, the word *home*
flashes like a traffic-light whenever I
see a seabound wing glint, then disappear, another
catching light. I welcome them
to this inland station, liking the way
they live by their hungry wits
on what they happen on, what happens. In
silence I walk this way to work and home again
like any native, under the bearing trees.

Hieroglyphic

Mid-February. Our first redwing blackbird
wheezes high up in the locust tree and I
call you out in your bathrobe to look,
listen. Your cup of coffee in the cold air
sends up propitiatory curls of steam, an
offering to the frost to soften its heart
and hurry home to mother; an offering
to the last sad carcasses of filthy snow
sprawled on any spot of all-day shade,
that they may take the heat and run,
praising in their own cold bodies
light, fluency and light, those
shape-shifters from way back. Your eyes
follow my finger to the bunched small blackness
in a crosshatch of twigs that haven't yet
begun to swell with a sense of things
to come. The redwing wheezes and briefly
clacks. Safe after riding storms and starlight
north from God knows where, he scans the brush
for a likely site, a soft spot near water,
where he'll flash his fiery epaulettes
and declare himself all spring and summer—
balancing a cattail while his mate broods
in hiding. I imagine a seedy, head-high field
brimming with their din and business, till
your shiver brings me back to where we stand
looking up at this solitary orator over our
skeletal world, this harbinger ahead of his
time. Cold, we go indoors again, satisfied
with this one sign for now—like archaeologists
who unearth a clay-caked single shard and
see in cracked turquoise a scallop-wing come
clear, and know a whole civilization lies
sleeping beneath their feet.

Daughter Lying Awake

Absence takes me heartsick
to my father's bony arms:
we make slow circles together.

The spider-plant shines in secret;
ferns fashion a green bedroom
where I dream his goodnight kiss,

living behind closed doors
with my dolls, my deep
amazement, and the strange

sad names of my dolls:
Hope, Heartsease, Love-
Lies-Bleeding.

March: the sharp sunlight
whittles exact shadows,
polishing platinum claws.

Grandfather's dead, he tells me,
sewing a shroud of words.
We'll go away together. Home

is the smell of lamb chops
and apples sweetening the kitchen;
mother's tears between the sheets.

Something is coming into leaf,
staining my window blind green:
nothing can stop that bleeding.

Something is flowing upwards
toward the clear heads of the crocuses
like music in the dark.

My daisy, he says, *my buttercup daughter,*
eyebright, my wild geranium, my
light mist in the morning. His

music. I turn my face to the wall
that's deaf to anything:
I try to sleep.

Traveller

He's ten, travelling alone for the first time—
by bus to the city. He settles an empty seat
and waves out at where I stand on the footpath
waiting for him to be taken, barely a shadow
grinning behind smoked glass. To his eyes
I'm a dim figure far off, smiling and waving
in a sea of traffic. Behind me the blinding sun
melts down the black back of hills
across the Hudson. For all there is to say
we are deaf to one another
and despatch our love in shrugs and pantomime
until he gives thumbs-up and the bus
sighs shut, shuddering away from me. He mouths
words I can't understand; I smile back
regardless, blowing a kiss through the air that
starts to stretch and empty between us. Alone,
he stares out a while, admiring his height
and speed, then reads two chapters of *The Dark
Is Rising*. When the real dark leaches in
he sees nothing but the huge loom
of a hill, the trees' hooded bulk and
come-hithering shadow. He tries to curl up
in sleep but sleep won't come. He presses
one cheek flat against the cold black glass
and peers out past his own faint ghost
up at the sky, as any night-time traveller
would—as Henry Hudson must have, sailing his
Half Moon past Poughkeepsie, already smelling
the Pacific. My son seeks the stars he knows:
Orion's belt, his sword, his dog
fall into place, make sense of the dark
above his voyaging. *When I found him*, he says,
I felt at home. And fell asleep. I imagine him
asleep in his rocky seat there,

like that wet sea-boy dozing at mast-head,
whose lullaby the whole Atlantic hums
in the lull between storms, the brief
peace between battles, no land in sight.

Walking Fall

When we enter the woods off Route 17
you walk ahead of me, your cranberry cardigan
brightening among the spectral shades
and flush of late October. The woods are emptying
around us to the bone, a blaze of tall angels
moulting slowly, setting the secular air
on fire. Still green are the slim spears of
mountain laurel; bunchberries glow bloodred
in the cloudcapped silent afternoon. You shine
among phantoms, listening to a dry scuffle
in the underbrush: *whitethroat*, I whisper,
touching your side, and you give me
out of the crushed leaf you hold to my nose
sassafras, a pungent sweetness foaming
at the mouth. We take these words
to heart, and all that, rooted, bides
its time inside them. Solid beech-bark grey,
the womb of a yellowjacket nest hangs
planetary among a thinning shimmer of
star-leaves—paper ghost of a humming
cell-brim summer stored with spring, a bushel
of sleeping queens we leave in peace. Kneeling,
I pluck a fan of small hemlock-green leaves
and bring them up from the dead for you, snapping
one drily open. The sharp remedial rush
of wintergreen comes over us: we close our eyes
and hold our breath, living inside this
bladed fragrance, and I remember the vein of
frozen snow glinting in the burly oak-log
I split last spring, how it fiercely sizzled
when the flame licked it. We could live here,
I imagine, safe on a hill out of harm's way, where
everything is of some blessed essence
and quickens breath, winter coming on and the trees'

great heads lifting for the light, the light that
blazes first, then burrows deeper in until,
skeletoned in snowlight, trees will stand
like x-rays of themselves, roots shuddering under
in artesian sleep. Turned back the way we came,
we tell each other what separately we saw:
the secret ivory swell of mushrooms
mounting one another in a poisonous ring; a last
black dangle of wild grapes; blue smoke; the
red-tail hawk above it all, idoling
a dead pine; and faintly blazing a trail
ahead of you through silence, a female
pheasant, unruffled, walking home alone.

All Souls' Morning

Rain splatting wet leaves; citrine light; the cat
scratching the sofa; the house dead quiet
but for the furnace thumping in the cellar; that man,
my neighbour, out on Locust Road as he is each morning,
whatever the weather, walking his dog. Bent shoulders,
heavy head, a cherry leash dangling
from a pale hand, his dog the dark tan of oakleaves
when they turn and hang and enter the depths
of winter. I see a huge patience in his stoop, in
the ghostly cigarette limp between his lips, the stiff
tilt of his head, the treadle action of his passage, the
orange surprise of a golf umbrella blossoming
from one fist, the loll of the dog by his side as they
return up Locust, keen to be in again from the cold
wet day that's breaking round them. I'm thinking how,
bound to one another, they've been at this
for years, when my father comes leaning as he always did
up Clareville Road, not far from where he's buried, bent
against the bitter wind that tunnelled it
in winter, his black umbrella furled, our small black
terrier, Brandy, straining the leash towards home
where my mother fusses the tea together. Five o'clock
and Dublin's dark already, being November. Fat raindrops
scud the wind and mix with his lost thoughts
as he hastens after his dog and home to the wife
who, when he leaves her behind, will run aground with grief
at being no one in the world. This is the bottom line: we
button our habits to the chin and set out, any weather,
walking with death. Here I hear a bluejay's screech
rattle the skeleton of our locust tree. The road
beyond my window is empty again. Rain gives way
to skybright weather, grey aquarium light
making luminous the air, coating dark tarmac
with mirrorpools of periwinkle blue. The risen wind

tides among survivor leaves, and a swallow-flock of dead ones
joyrides Locust Road, cold no more, borne off. *All night,*
you said when we wakened warm by one another, *I was*
seeing shapes widen round the room, hearing them
whisper in the wall. And this minute my hungry children come
clattering to the kitchen for breakfast. The house quickens.

Totem

All Souls' over, the roast seeds eaten, I set
on a backporch post our sculpted pumpkin under the weather,
warm still for November. Night and day it gapes
in at us through the kitchen window, going soft
in the head. Sleepwalker-slow, a black rash of ants
harrows this hollowed globe, munching the pale peach
flesh, sucking its seasoned last juices dry. In a
week, when the ants and humming flies are done, only
a hard remorseless light drills and tenants it
through and through. Within, it turns mould-black
in patches, stays days like this while the weather
takes it in its shifty arms: wide eye-spaces shine,
the disapproving mouth holds firm. Another week,
a sad leap forward: sunk to one side so an eye-socket's
almost blocked, it becomes a monster of its former
self. Human, it would have rotted beyond unhappiness and
horror to some unspeakable subject state—its nose
no more than a vertical hole, the thin bridge of amber
between nose and mouth in ruins. The other socket opens
wider than ever: disbelief. It's all downhill
from here: knuckles of sun, peremptory steady fingers
of frost, strain all day and night at it, cracking
the rind, kneading the knotted fibres free. The crown
with its top-knot mockery of stalk caves in; the skull
buckles; the whole head drips tallowy tears: the end
is in sight. In a day or two it topples on itself
like ruined thatch, pus-white drool spidering
from the corner of the mouth and worming its way
down the body-post. All dignity to the winds, it bows its
bogeyman face of dread to the inevitable. And now, November
almost out, it is in the bright unseasonable sunshine
a simmer of pulp, a slow bake, amber shell speckled
chalk-grey with lichen. Light strikes and strikes
its burst surfaces: it sags, stays at the end of its

brief tether—a helmet of dark circles, death caul. Here
is the last umbilical gasp, everybody's nightmare parent,
the pitiless system rubbing our noses in it. But
pity poor lantern-head with his lights out, glob
by greasy glob going back where he came from. As each
seed-shaped drop falls free, it catches and clutches
for one split second the light. When the pumpkin
lapses to our common ground at last—where a white
swaddle of snow will fold it in no time from sight—
I try to take in the empty space it's left
on top of the wooden post: it is that empty space.

Winter Morning, Twelve Noon

Light snags in January branches. On the sunstark
living-room wall two starlings are a writing
smear of shadow. Out in the snow a scarlet cardinal
stands heroned on one delicate stem of a leg: he
flutters the other as a cat does
after water, then folds it gingerly into
the glowing stove of his breast. Our striped cat
sits statued at the window staring out, her
smokepale eyes steady as a sniper's: when a
chickadee scratches for a landing on glass, she
shivers, coils, and springs straight up at it,
then slides back stiff as a stick and hits
the sill-geranium, snapping it at the stem. In one
wiry bound she's up the stairs, out from under
my shout of anger. The whole plant-shelf trembles.

I see it has begun to snow again, a slow
featherdown drift that glints, sun-stippled,
through slashblue tatters of cloud. I can hear
the cardinal start to sing in hiding—beguiled
by sunlight or feeling another season shake itself,
half a continent away, from sleep. It is his
spring song, each note clear as water falling
in fiery drops off eaves: I can tell his desperate heart
is in it. The heavy clouds close over, shadows
vanish, the sweet bird stops, the grey containing air

grows still. I set the broken stem in a glass
of water: white rootlets curl and catch, as the water
catches, what light there is. What light
there is. Out at the feeder the speckled
starlings are squabbling; a small flock of children
scatters past my window, snowsuited and screaming
with joy. In Sweden, in December, I hear they wait

impatient for the first big snow
to brighten their all-day dusk. I imagine them
standing bareheaded under it in happy groups
at last, shaking hands with one another, holding their
eager faces up like urns, like fresh leaves, to those
slow crystals of cold, those flakes of light.

Jewel Box

Your jewel box of white balsa strips
and bleached green Czechoslovakian rushes
stands open where you keep it shelved
in the bathroom. Morning and evening
I see you comb its seawrack tangle of shell,
stone, wood, glass, metal, bone, seed
for the bracelet, earring, necklace, brooch
or ring you need. Here's brass from Nepal,
a bangle of African ivory and chased silver
for your wrist, a twist of polished scarlet
sandalwood seeds gleaming like the fossil
tears of some long-gone exotic bird
with ruby crest, sapphire claws. Adriatic
blue, this lapis lazuli disc will brighten
the pale of your throat, and on this small
alabaster seal-ring the phantom of light
inscribes a woman tilting an amphora, clear
as day, almost as old as Alexander. To
the ebony velvet brim of your hat you'll pin
a perfect oval of abalone, a dark-whorled
underwater sheen to guide us to work
this foggy February morning. We'll leave
your nest of brightness in the bathroom
between the mirror and the laundry-basket
where my dirty shirts sprawl like
drunks among your skirts and blouses. Lace-
work frills and rainbow silk pastels, your panties
foam over the plastic brim, and on the shower-rail
your beige and talc-white bras dangle by one strap
like the skinned Wicklow rabbits I remember
hanging from hooks outside the victuallers'
big windows. We've been domesticated strangely,
love, according to our lights: when you
walk by me now, naked and not quite dry

from the shower, I flatten my two hands
on your wet flank and wonder at the tall
column of flesh you are, catching the faint
morning light that polishes you pale as
alabaster. You're warm, and stay a moment
still like that, as though we were two planets
pausing in their separate orbits, pendant,
on the point of crossing. For one pulse-stroke
they take stock of their bodies
before returning to the journey. Dressed,
you select a string of chipped amber
to hang round your neck, a pair of star-shaped
earrings, a simple ring of jet black,
lustrous onyx. Going down the dark stairs and
out to the fogbound street, you light my way.

Lizards in Sardinia

I miss our lizards. The one who watched us
lunch on the rocks, half of him
sandstone brown, the other half neat rings
of neon avocado. He moved his head in
wary jerks, like a small bird. Unblinking,
his stillness turned him stone. When he
shifted, whiptail, his whole length flowed
like water. Those reptile eyes of his
took in a world we couldn't see, as he
paused in the dragon-roar of sunlight till
his blood boiled again, then lit out for shadows
and an age of fragrance. The other one
who'd lost his tail and stumped about, still
quick as a lizard, vanishing behind the trunk
of the eucalyptus. Two who scuttled circles,
tail of one clamped fast in the other's
mouth: courtship, you hoped, as they dervished
among the piebald, finger-slim, fallen leaves
and rustled into infinity—a flash,
an absence—minute leftovers with molten brains,
escapees when their sky-high brothers bowed
cloud-scraping heads and bit the dust, leaving
the wrecked armadas of their ribs
for us to wonder at. Or that plump one
squatting beside me at the edge of the steel
and turquoise bay you rose from dripping light
and smiling in my direction: unblemished emerald
down half his length, the rest opaque and
dull, we thought, until we saw the envelope
of old skin he was shedding, under which
jewel-bright he blazed our breath away—like
the one I dreamt when my father died, big
as an iguana and the colour of greaseproof paper
till I saw him gleam and be a newborn beast of

jade and flame who stood there mildly casting
his old self off and shining. Those afternoons
after we'd made love I lay quite still
along your back, blood simmering, and saw
your splayed palms flatten on the white sheet
like a lizard's, while we listened, barely
breathing, to the wind whiffle the eucalyptus
leaves against the window, our new world
steadying around us, its weather settled.

A Closer Look

for Peter Fallon

Simply that I'm sick of our wars and
the way we live, wasting everything we touch
with our hands, lips, tongues, crowding
the earth with early graves, blind
to the bright little nipples of rain
that simmer on willow twigs, amber shoots
of the stumped willow itself a burning bush
on the scalloped hem of the ice-pond. So
I'm turning to winter beasts instead, their
delicate razor's-edge economies as they
shift for themselves between dens, migrant
homebodies like the souls we used to have,
leaving behind them in the shallow snow
their signatures, the thing itself, illiterate
signs that say no more than *We were here*
and mean it: handprints, footprints, midnight-
mahogany blossoms of shit, citrus
and mustardgreen swirls of piss that brighten
the eye-numbing, one blank world. Porcupine,
possum, raccoon, skunk, fox—behold them
combing the cold land for a bite, not just
taking for granted their world as it comes
and goes. They wear the weather like a shawl
and follow their noses through a sphere
of sudden death and instant satisfactions: they
lie in the sunlit pit of sleep, or the worm
of hunger winds his luminous tail to rouse
and send them coldly forth, sniffing the wind
the way lovers browse word by word by word
first letters for what stays salted
and aromatic between the lines. It isn't
innocence I find in them, but a fathoming
depth of attention anchored in the heart, in its
whorl of blood and muscle beating round—the way

they traffic between frosted starlight and the
gleamy sphere of berries and last apples, between
storm in the big cloud-bearing boughs
and the narrow breath of earthworm and beetle
barely stirring the dead leaves; now all
quivering dash, nerves purring, now the wildfire
flash of pain that lays them, an open secret,
low. I try to make my hopeless own of this, to
sense in myself their calm unthreading
between brisk teeth or busy mycelian fingers, breaking,
as we will, down to our common ground, the whole story
starting over in the old language: air first, then
ooze, then the solid lie of things, then fire,
a further twist, begin again. Making do.

Men Roofing
for Seamus Heaney

Bright burnished day, they are laying fresh roof down
on Chicago Hall. Tight cylinders of tarred felt-paper
lean against one another on the cracked black shingles
that shroud those undulant ridges. Two squat drums
of tar-mix catch the light: a fat canister of gas
gleams between a heap of old tyres and a paunchy
plastic sack, beer-bottle green. A TV dish-antenna
stands propped to one side, a harvest moon, cocked
to passing satellites and steadfast stars. Gutters
overflow with starlings, lit wings and whistling throats
going like crazy. A plume of blue smoke feathers up
out of a pitch-black cauldron, making the air fragrant
and medicinal, as my childhood's was, with tar. Overhead
against the gentian sky a sudden first flock whirls
of amber leaves and saffron, quick as breath, fine
as origami birds. Watching from a window opposite,
I see a man in a string vest glance up at these exalted
leaves, kneel to roll a roll of tar-felt flat; another
tilts a drum of tar-mix till a slow bolt of black silk
oozes, spreads. One points a silver hose and conjures
from its nozzle a fretted trembling orange lick
of fire. The fourth one dips to the wrist in the green sack
and scatters two brimming fistfuls of granite grit:
broadcast, the bright grain dazzles on black. They pause,
straighten, study one another—a segment done. I can see
the way the red-bearded one in the string vest grins and
slowly whets his two stained palms along his jeans; I see
the one who cast the grit walk to the roof-edge, look over,
then, with a little lilt of the head, spit contemplatively
down. What a sight between earth and air they are, drenched
in sweat and sunlight, relaxed masters for a moment
of all our elements. Here is my image, given, of the world
at peace: men roofing, taking pains to keep the weather
out, simmering in ripe Indian-summer light, winter

on their deadline minds. Briefly they stand balanced
between our common ground and nobody's sky, then move
again to their appointed tasks and stations, as if they
were amazing strangers come to visit for a short spell our
familiar shifty climate of blown leaves, birdspin. Odorous,
their column of lazuli smoke loops up from the dark
heart of their mystery; and they ply, they intercede.

Lesson

The needles he's using
are thick as chopsticks. Proud
of his mastery—to be at nine
his father's father in this art—
he shows me how to loop, draw off,
draw under, begin again. I fumble,
all thumbs, till he takes me
in hand, clicking and slowly twisting
the turquoise needles, with patience
explaining each new move. After
many jabs and draggings I've one row
done, and hand the ball of thick tan wool
back to him, needles sticking askew like
stripped tailfeathers. We're both relieved.

At his age I helped my mother
by balancing hanks of wool on my hands,
arms outstretched like a fisherman's. Her
fingers twirled, running colour
round and round between us, the ball
in her left hand growing thicker and
thicker. Lulled by the monotonous
brisk rhythm of our give and take, I'd
almost fall asleep on my feet, my thumbs
dipping and rising and dipping
as the wool wriggled over, subdued
to a steady heartbeat of attention,
a drowsy fullness, satisfaction.

He goes on counting stitches
on his own—each loop lightly tipped
with the needle's beak, ticked off.
Behind us, I imagine, in a shadowed
corner, three women are working wool

as if our lives depended on it. And
at the far side of the fire, out of my son's
sight, my mother sits in her younger self
intently knitting. She does not lift
her eyes from the task, and the silent
strict sisters do not lift theirs.

Pieces of Kate

Eleven
Her whole body flowing
into her beginner's
melodies and scales.

Her breakfast talk's
all teachers, boys, French
verbs, what her friends

are wearing: electric green
eye-liner, purple tights
spangled with sequins. Panic

and shadows, her dreams all
end in her mother's voice,
a swan at lift-off, some sort

of illumination. She laughs
these frost-bitten mornings
at how her breath smokes

in the car's cold air. When she
leaves and her friends are watching
her kiss barely brushes

my cheek, though alone
in the kitchen she'll suddenly
hug me hard, or giggle, shivering,

at the way I nibble
the dip in her freckled neck
on the edge of sleep.

Twelve
She visits week-ends. Frayed
by the strain of the distance between us
her voice stays wary.

Curled cat-like on the quilt
her twelve wise years stare past me
to the window, where light

thickens to a violet wash: the world
melting before our eyes. Quickly she
kisses me goodnight, then buries herself

in *The Never Ending Story*. At the far
side of the closed door I listen
to her music-box, its white dancer

circling and circling: the tinny tune
slows, falters, falls silent
in the middle of a phrase. Last year,

each school-day after breakfast I'd
help her into her winter jacket. Then,
heads bent in wondering silence

we'd walk across the hard white
grass to the car, through a sudden
clamorous, out-of-the-bushes, bursting up of birds.

Thirteen
Her Junior High School graduation:
she's singing alone
in front of the lot of us—

her voice soprano,
surprising, almost
a woman's. The *Our Father*

in French, the new language
making her strange, out
there, full-fledged and

ready for anything. Sitting
together—her mother, her
father—we can hear

the racket of traffic
shake the main streets
of Jersey City as she sings

Deliver us from evil,
and I wonder can she see me
in the dark here, years

from belief, on the edge
of tears. Doesn't matter. She
doesn't miss a beat, stays

in time, in tune, while
into our common silence I whisper
Sing, love; sing your heart out!

In Winter: Three Women

1.
One meets you on the run
through early morning intervals
of light and shade.

Feathering pods of her breath
burst on the iron air. Her breasts
make two small dents against cotton.

Her heart, you see, beats time
between you, a stuttering
tongue. Lit pimples of sweat

stipple her forehead and flushed cheeks,
burning the bridge behind you. Cold
and going your own way, flagrant

comrade, you taste that mortal salt.

2.
I'm forced to find in this other woman
winter abiding. Shunted pillar to post
in a cloud of panic, she whispers
she has something to tell us but
no time to piece the impossible
words together. Poor body solitary,
in broken flight from every terrible
shred of evidence, she gapes in whatever
glass she passes: stunned eyes question
the face she faces: *Dear God can that
be me?* Cold to the hopeless bone
I turn away and wait for her
to catch up with me again, to put
her cradle arm again in mine.

3.

You are bent over the empty grate
the moment we stumble in from cold
snowlight curdling to early dark
outside. Kneeling, you wrench
dry box-slats to bits and lay them
on quick-twisted wreaths of newspaper
and fumble with matches. Dogs
in the open dark start to bark
at the rising frostwhite face
of the full moon in its net
of hemlock, and all around your body
big spirited petals of light
begin to throb and glow from
the fine leaping wonder of fire. Slowly
you straighten to watch, holding
open your ashy hands stretched out
like offerings, your whole particular
body solving and dissolving
in this rich crackling flux you've made
for us to breathe in
warmly, of light, of shade.

Homelight

Six or so this January morning
under the streetlamp where Wing and Locust
meet, a maple tree splays its shadow
over snow in the front garden. The house
around me sinks deeper into sleep. I'm
back after two weeks away.
                              Dublin
was wearing its air of winter damp. On
Clareville Road a skin of frost winked
like mica in the morning. The back garden
green and bony, the single appletree
I trimmed in brimming summer a skeleton
decked with wrinkled amulets. One rose
sprang pink, straight-stemmed, brilliant,
and a yellow burst of winter jasmine
fired the concrete wall with stars. Our
neighbour's garden offered winter plum
in blossom: a fragile spread umbrella
of white lace, mocking snow.
                              Those
first dazzled days I knew nothing but
birthlight, the place native, original,
and clinging like skin to some speechless
centre in me, a small sphere of self
that weathers change the way the stars
bear daylight. Days bristled with familiars:
blue shreds of sky seen from the scullery
window; torn cloud ragging the roof
of the coalshed; a plump thrush
picking through the amber pulp
of rotten apples. I lived again on
the razor's-edge between rain and shine,
catching the rubber kiss of tyres against
wet tarmac; the noon-thick shadows of cats

ghosting between deep green privet hedges
and lance-head railings; sparrows squabbling
at the makeshift feeder. Briefly each
was illuminated.
                    Nights I'd lie awake
to the repeated, remembered wheeze
of traffic changing gears outside my
bedroom window, hear the midnight singers
wake archaic echoes, sowing dragon sweetness
on the road to Sundrive. I woke to
the dawn penny-jig of milk-bottles
in the hollow porches. The morning's
fleet lucidity prised open every
crack: puddles of standing water shivered
into a million windows when the light
hit and ran; rose-hips were glowing
in the winter solstice.
                    I was born
to morning light templing the back wall
I clambered as a boy and perched, king
of my castle of air and briary prospects,
and saw the big eye-taking world brood
and blazon right there in my own
back garden. I've only come to know this again
when it's time to leave for the airport
to fly to my rented home of snow: sharp
green starts of daffodils are daring
the air, darting infant fingers from the dark
ground on which my father's house—exactly
as old as I am—stands.
                    Back here
in Poughkeepsie and the grip of winter
I draw the blinds and watch the iced-up
iron dark dissolve, say goodbye to green,
and welcome snowlight, its terminal
sheen and shiver. Welcome the crusty crunching
of hard snow under my boots when I walk, mornings,

over our garden to the car, while you stand, home-
body, behind the double-glazed storm door
in your white bathrobe. You wave at me
passing in a cloud of exhaust and waving back
at you framed there, there where we live
in this brief-lit, but lit, ring of winter.

Four Deer

Four deer lift up their lovely heads to me
in the dusk of the golf course I plod across
towards home. They're browsing the wet grass
the snow has left and, statued, stare at me
in deep silence and I see whatever light there is
gather to glossy pools in their eight mild,
barely curious but wary eyes. When one at a time
they bend again to feed, I can hear the crisp
moist crunch of the surviving grass
between their teeth, imagine the slow lick of a tongue
over whickering lips. They've come from the unlit
winter corners of their fright to find
a fresh season, this early gift, and stand
almost easy at the edge of white snow islands and
lap the grey-green sweet depleted grass. About them
hangs an air of such domestic sense, the comfortable
hush of folk at home with one another, a familiar
something I sense in spite of the great gulf of strangeness
we must look over at each other. Tails flicker
white in thickening dusk and I feel their relief at
the touch of cold snow underfoot while their faces
nuzzle grass, as if, like birds, they had crossed
unspeakable vacant wastes with nothing but hunger
shaping their brains and driving them from leaf to
dry leaf, sour strips of bark, under a thunder of guns
and into the cold comfort of early dark. I've seen
their straight despairing lines cloven in snowfields
under storm, an Indian file of famished natives, poor
unprayed-for wanderers through blinding chill, seasoned
castaways in search of home ports, which they've found
at last, here on winter's verge between our houses and
their trees. All of a sudden, I've come too close. Moving
as one mind they spring in silent waves
over the grass, then crack snow with sharp hard

snaps, lightfooting it into the sanctuary of a pine grove
where they stand looking back at me, a deer-shaped
family of shadows against the darker arch of trees and
this rusting dusk. When silence settles over us again
and they bow down to browse, the sound of grass being
lipped, bitten, meets me across the space between us. Close
enough for comfort, they see we keep, instinctively, our
distance, sharing this air where a few last shards of
daylight still glitter in little meltpools or spread a skin
of brightness on the ice, the ice stiffening towards midnight
under the clean magnesium burn of a first star.

At Home in Winter

1.
We sit across from one another
in front of the fire, the big logs
clicking and hissing. Outside
is bitter chill: locust branches
grow brittle as crystal. You're
sewing a skirt, your pursed mouth
full of pins, head swimming with
Greek and Latin. You frown
so not to swallow any pins when
you try to smile at me
slumped under the *TLS* and bewailing
the seepage of my days, the way
my life runs off like water, yet
inexplicably happy at this moment
balanced between us like a tongue
of flame skiving a pine log and seeming
to breathe, its whole involuntary life
spent giving comfort. It would
be a way to live: nothing
going to waste; such fullness
taking off; warm space;
a fragrance. Now the sight of you
bending to baste the blue skirt
before you pleat and sew the waistband in
enters and opens inside me, so
for a second or two I am an empty centre,
nothing at all,
then back to this home truth
unchanged: you patiently taking
one thing at a time as I can't
and all the while your head beating with
hexameters and foreign habits. I go on
reading in silence, as if I hadn't

been startled into another life
for a fiery instant, inhaling the faintly
resinated air that circulates
like blood between our two bodies.

2.
Blown in from the noonwhite bite of snow
I find the whole house fragrant as a haycock
with the soup you've stirred up, its spirit
seeping into closets, curtains, bedrooms—
a prosperous mix of chicken stock, carrots,
garlic, onion, thyme. All morning
you've wreathed your head in it, and now
you turn to me like a minor deity of earth
and plenty, hands dipped to the wrist
in the flesh of vegetables, your fingers
trailing threads from the mound of bones
glistening on the counter-top. You stand
at the edge of a still life—glazed
twists of onion skin, papery garlic sacs,
bright carrot stumps, grass-green delicate
stems of parsley, that little midden
of bones—and I behold
how in the middle of my daily life
a sober snow-bound house
can turn to spirit of chicken, air a
vegetable soul, and breathe on me. You
turn back to the stove, wooden spoon
still steaming, and say
in no time now we'll sit and eat.

Morning: The Twenty-Second of March

All the green things in the house
on fire with greenness. The trees
in the garden take their naked ease
like *Demoiselles d'Avignon*. We came
awake to the spider-plant's crisp shadow
printing the pillowcase
between us. Limp fingers of steam
curl auspiciously from the cup
of tea I've brought you, and a blue-jay
screeches blue murder beyond the door.
In a painting over the bed
five tea-coloured cows stand
hock-deep in water at the broad
bend of a river—small smoothback stones
turtling its near margin. A brace
of leafy branches leans over it
from the far bank, where the sun
spreads an open field like butter,
while the cows bend down to the
dumbfound smudge of their own faces
in the flat, metallic water. And here
this minute at the bristle tip
of the Scotch pine, a cardinal
starts singing: seven compound metal notes
equal in beat, then silence, then
again the identical seven. Between
the sighs the cars and pick-ups make,
relenting for the curve with a little
gasp of gears, we hear over the road
among the faintly flesh pink
limbs and glow of the apple orchard
a solitary dove throating three sweet
mournful *Om*, then falling silent, then
—our life together hesitating in this gap

of silence, slipping from us and becoming
nothing we know in the swirl that has
no past, no future, nothing
but the pure pulse-shroud of light, the
dread *here-now*—reporting thrice again
its own silence. The cup of tea
still steams between your hands
like some warm offering or other
to the nameless radiant vacancy at the window,
this stillness in which we go on happening.

Conjunctions

1.

In the cold dome of the college observatory
I wait my turn to lay an eye on
Halley's Comet. For a minute I'm a watcher
of the skies in total silence, my whole self
swimming the shaft of the telescope, blunt as
a big gun, out across the dark to our one and
only rendezvous. It's a faint milky bristling,
like the frizzled head of a small dandelion
gone to seed. Distinctly throbbing, sperm-like
and full of purpose in its journey, it seems as intimate
as the tick of my own pulse, though its far heart is
ice and a rage of lizard-green, sulphur, steel-blue,
its corona cloudy rose, riding into the light
of our world at biblical intervals, a hard fact, a sign
simply *out there*, meaning maybe nothing at all
or just what we make of it. But this once, at least,
I'm here to meet it, make its path cross mine, figuring
the unthinkable winter space between the lot of us—
those impossible distances and the uncanny, happy,
unrepeatable accident. This is all I see before
I step back out into our night glinting with chill
and see the sky an unreadable maze of stars, its sudden
comings and goings—brief white birds ablaze—and
under my boots the snow gleaming, hard as stone.

2.

A hard bright day, late February, you tell me
you're pregnant. The dead grass is scabbed with snow
and oozing a premature, deceptive thaw. We cross
at the lights on Raymond, holding hands against
the heavy traffic. You've been sick—your system
briefly poisoned, in a fist of fever by day, night-
sweats—and we worry it will make some dangerous

difference. I imagine this circumstantial creature
taking shape inside you, our quick derivative
yet already someone separate and strange, a pulse
of difference in the dark uncharted space
you've offered up, a hurried little heartbeat
syncopate with yours, compounding hearts. It's early
days yet, but you've opened my weather eye
for signs—for a warm corner in the ice-wind
rattling last year's locust pods like maracas, a
flash of frantic amber in the stark branches
of the willow, a few lemon flecks on the goldfinch,
or a hoarse wheeze from the first redwing blackbird
to claim home ground among the mazy brush and cattails
out back. These live signs will wind around you
like planets, love, while you grow more than yourself
at the season's weathery, fragrant, unprevailing
heart. And on the outskirts I will bend to listen
to that other heart kicking its mysteries, before
our common ground and gravity, in the enlarging dark.

3.
I'm in the dark, going home fast
along the Palisades, the night roaring and flashing
with the cars I pass, that pass me, all our lives at hazard
on the simple spin of a wheel, locked anonymously into
this meteor shower above the legal speed limit. I've
been handing over to Joan the children, as happens
every other week-end: we meet at a gas-station and
deliver our children up—lovingly, to take the sting
out of it—to one another. I'm thinking about this,
about the way my words can't catch it yet but
about must, and about must go—trying to be true
to the unavoidable ache in the grain of healing,
trying to boil the big words down to size—when a fox
lights out of hiding in the highway's grassy island
and arrows across the road before me, a rust-
gold flash from dark to dark. In that split second I catch

the compass-point of his nose, the quilled tip
of ears *in áirde*, the ruddering lift of a tail as he
streams by my sight, and I only have time to
lift my instinct's foot from the gas, clap hands, cry
"Fox!" in fright or invocation and he's gone, under
the metal fence, into the trees, home free. But all the
rest of the way home I hold him in my mind: a body
burning to its outer limits of bristle with this
moment, creature eyes alive with purpose, child
of time and impeccable timing
who has cometed across my vacant dark, a flow of
leaf-rust and foxy gold, risk-taker
shooting sure as a bird into the brush
with every hair in place, a splice
of apprehension, absolute, and pure indifference. He
is only getting on with his life, I know,
but engraved on my brain for good now
is his cave shape at full stretch, caught
in the brief blaze of my headlights
just like that . . . and still running.

Notes

Page 40: *Raeburn's Skater* refers to a painting called *The Rev. Robert Walker Skating on Duddingston Loch* by the Scottish artist Sir Henry Raeburn (1756–1823).

Page 76: Vermeer's *A Girl Asleep*, in the Metropolitan Museum of Art, New York.

Page 78: The painting described in the second stanza is a conflation of a number of works by the brothers Job and Gerritt Berckheyde and Jan van der Heyde. The conflation was unintentional, the result of poor memory.

Page 83: The English explorer Henry Hudson thought he'd found the chimeral Northwest Passage when he sailed up what is now the Hudson River. By the time he'd reached a point a bit north of Poughkeepsie, he realised his mistake.

Page 84: "that wet sea-boy" is borrowed from one of the King's lines in *Henry the Fourth*, Part Two (III, i, 27).

Page 99: Chicago Hall is an academic building that houses the departments of foreign languages in Vassar College.

Page 102: The three sisters are the Fates. Their statue in St. Stephen's Green, Dublin, was particularly in my mind.

Page 118: Section 3: the quotation, *"about must..."*, is from Donne, *Satire* III ("On a huge hill, / Cragged and steep, Truth stands, and hee that will / Reach her, about must, and about must goe").

Page 119: The Irish phrase *in áirde* (*erect*) is taken from the children's song *An Maidrín Rua* (*The Little Fox*).